ADOPTION SAVED MY LIFE

An Inspiring Story of Success.
(Second Edition)

DOMINIC MUNAFO

with

CURTIS FLORENCE

DOMINIC MUNAFO

Dreamstone Publishing

www.dreamstonepublishing.com

In conjunction with

Florence Publishing © 2016

www.florencepublishing.wordpress.com/

Copyright © 2016 Dreamstone Publishing, Florence Publishing, Curtis Florence and Dominic Munafo

Second Edition May 2016

Editing and Cover Graphics by Kim Lambert, Dreamstone Publishing.

All rights reserved.

No parts of this work may be copied without the author's permission

ISBN 13: 978-1-925499-04-9

DISCLAIMER

The information, strategies, concepts, techniques and suggestions in this book are of a general nature only, and do not constitute, and are not intended as a substitute for, professional or individual advice in any way. You should consult with the appropriate qualified professionals (including psychologists, psychiatrists, counsellors, medical practitioners and other healthcare providers, financial advisers, and legal advisers) and seek your own independent professional advice relating to your particular circumstances and needs.

Although the author and the publisher have made every effort to ensure that the contents of this book were accurate at press time, the author and the publisher do not represent or warrant their accuracy. The author and the publisher are not responsible for any disruption, loss or damage (including indirect or consequential damages) suffered by any party as a result of or in relation to the use of this book. To the extent permitted by law, the author and the publisher exclude any liability (including liability for negligence or other default) to any party for any disruption, loss or damage (including indirect or consequential damages) arising from or in relation to the use of this book.

> "Everything that is really **great** and **inspiring** is created by the **individual** who can labor in **freedom**."
>
> -Albert Einstein

DEDICATION

This book is dedicated to my mom Cheryl - you are the best mom a man could ever have. It takes a real woman to raise a child, not just to make one. To my stepdad Jimmy for everything you did for me!

To my the rest of my adoptive family, without you all I would not have had the courage to try and make a difference in my own life and for people all over the world

To my wife Doris, thank you for being my support and encouragement.

Table of Contents

DISCLAIMER iii

DEDICATION v

FOREWORD viii

INTRODUCTION x

CHAPTER ONE – AN INTRODUCTION TO MY FAMILY TREE 1

CHAPTER TWO – GROWING UP 15

    THE MAGIC OF SURVIVAL 19

    LIFE LESSONS 24

CHAPTER THREE - THE ICE CREAM KING 33

    OVERCOME YOUR FEARS 39

    THIS IS YOUR LIFE CHANGE 41

CHAPTER FOUR – DOMINIC'S NOTEBOOK 43

   SUPPORT FOR DOMINIC'S NOTEBOOK 55

CHAPTER FIVE – LIVE YOUR DREAMS 59

THANK YOU 69

ABOUT THE AUTHOR 82

   CONNECT WITH DOMINIC 83

HOW YOU CAN HELP DOMINIC'S NOTEBOOK 84

FOREWORD

It has been my utmost pleasure becoming a friend with Dominic. I met him through Facebook as he entered a contest called "This is your life change." I was there to support another friend but I was compelled by Dominic's story and positivity.

He was the only other person I saw in the contest that spoke volumes to pursuing his dreams. I soon began interacting with him because as you know, like attracts like, and I personally love like-minded people.

I was in the midst of pursuing my own dreams as an author and a speaker and he began to inspire me. I could tell right away that he was a go-getter and I could also tell that great things were destined for his future. His story compelled me even more when I found out he was adopted and had dedicated his life to helping kids in the foster care system and any others in need.

I have two adopted children of my own and have fostered many others so it was a true honor for me when I was asked to work on this exceptional story.

He is such a great example of righteousness and I know his story will inspire you as much as it inspired me. When you connect with Dominic Munafo, whether it is business or personal, you are getting sincerity, loyalty, dependability, inspiration and best of all, love.

Curtis Florence

INTRODUCTION

My name is Dominic Anthony Munafo and I am living proof that dreams absolutely do come true. I want everyone reading this to know that you can go from being an ordinary person to an extraordinary person if you so choose to take action and dedicate yourself to a worthy ideal.

When you look at me I want you to see yourself because I am you. Greatness is not only intended for a select few, it is a promised option to all who are willing to pursue it.

My life has been filled with immense love and a wealth of experiences that have inspired me to make a difference in the world. As far back as I can remember I have always wanted to inspire people to follow their path to happiness. I believe that we all experience things in life that can be used to help and inspire other people to find their dreams.

My life, of course is no exception to this golden rule. I want to be a voice for the voiceless, I believe that the world always needs a hero and it is you.

It is you who stand up and lead by example that makes the world we live in a better place.

It is your courage and bravery that brings about change in the world. It is how we stand up for what is right and resist what is wrong that empowers us. Remember those wrong deeds around us are only there to scare us away from our own path!

Never be afraid to lead by example; instead be afraid to follow in fear!

I'm a big admirer of Steve Harvey and I once heard him say that in order to get more out of life you have to "jump" for it. He, of course was speaking metaphorically and here's what I took from that. To "jump" would be the difference between living life to its fullest potential and simply existing.

In other words you have to take a huge leap of faith to achieve more in life. Trust me it is okay to "jump" because the whole world is out there waiting on you. Use your gifts to maximize your potential. Don't allow yourself to sit around watching everyone else achieve success. It's your time! Focus on nothing else but maximizing the moment. Each passing moment in time is a chance to make a difference in the world. Don't allow yourself to waste moment after moment stepping in other people's footprints; instead create your own! When you choose to carve out your own path in life the world seems to yield to your presence. Remember it's all for a higher plan so enjoy life and make the most of it.

Dominic Munafo

ADOPTION SAVED MY LIFE

DOMINIC MUNAFO

CHAPTER ONE – AN INTRODUCTION TO MY FAMILY TREE

On August 26th 1979 in Saranac Lake, New York a chubby little baby boy was born who was destined to become Dominic Anthony Munafo.

I was twice as adorable because I had two chubby cheeks and two chins to go along with them. Because of this everyone said I looked like the famous actor and comedian, Dom DeLuise.

I was born to young parents and I was my birth father's first born child. Since my birth father was in the military, his travels moved us from New York down to Aberdeen, Maryland.

My birth parents were a young military couple, struggling to keep it together in their relationship.

Financial and emotional hardships took over and their marriage was ending, so they decided that adoption was the best solution, and I was placed in foster care.

I'm not sure exactly how long I was in foster care, but I was fourteen months old when two angels, the Munafos, came into my life.

Joseph and Cheryl Munafo were two of the greatest blessings that I could have ever received at that moment in my life.

When the Munafo family picked me up from the foster care agency I couldn't really walk, like I should have been able to, because the shoes I had on were too small for me.

They immediately took me shopping for new shoes and, once those shoes got on my feet, I walked out of that store as if I was unstoppable. I spent an introductory period of time getting to know the Munafos and they soon agreed to adopt me.

They first took me home on October 28th 1980, just in time to experience my first Halloween.

ADOPTION SAVED MY LIFE

They gave me the name Dominic, after one of my father's close friends.

My father Joseph was the oldest of four children. They gave me the middle name of Anthony, after my father's father, Salvatore, who also had the same middle name. Grandpa Salvatore was from Maryland on the east coast, and his wife Edna was from California on the west coast.

My mother Cheryl's side of the family, the Huffmans, came from North Carolina and West Virginia, so needless to say, I was going to have a lot of love from all over the country.

I ended up being the youngest of all of the family's nephews and nieces, so that made me even more adorable.

My mother's parents were Richard and Virginia Huffman and mom was the youngest of eight children. It was a longtime dream of my parents to have a child of their own and I was blessed to be the answer to their prayers.

My adoption became a blessing for them and for me, but unfortunately life sometimes throws you a curve ball.

Unfortunately, Joseph and Cheryl severed their relationship when I was just a three year old toddler, but the fact that they were brought together to save my life, by adopting me, so that I was not left adrift in the system forever, was a sign in itself.

Joseph had troubles with addiction to pills, methadone and drinking, so it hindered him from being close with us. As I grew up, Joseph and I didn't get to have the best relationship but I never stopped loving him.

He, like everyone else, had his own flaws that put a damper on our relationship, but eventually time heals everything.

I was always mesmerized by Al Pacino, because Joseph used to dress just like him. I own just about every single Pacino movie - I believe it's because, in my subconscious, I was getting a few extra moments of quality time with Joseph, through the resemblance, even when he wasn't available.

Below, I'm going to share with you a picture of a poem I wrote about Joseph that was published in a book many years ago. At the time, Joseph was on a downward spiral and I wrote it because he was always on my mind.

The poem soon became a family tune and some still feel the beat of it to this very day.

> Stranded on a desserted island
> no more walking
> no more flying
> Drinking life away
> living for today.
> The pain inside is slowly rising
> a new day is on the horizon
> my body trembles when I'm dry
> and my brain is always complying
> I hit the bottle and keep on trying
> to take my mind away.
> Life is hard and I'm trying
> to keep on driving along
> I take a drink again
> because it's my only friend
> for it I depend.
> It's a place to run away
> I feel so irrate
> have a drink and stay up late
> thinking back contemplating
> doing some soul raiding.
> My brain gets twisted
> my heart beats rising
> feels like this boats capsizing
> please take this pain away.
>
> Written by: Dominic Munafo

Sadly enough Joseph passed away in 2009, shortly before his 60th birthday. Our relationship had just started to mend and he and I were supposed to spend our birthdays together. It would have been his 60th and my 30th birthday, but sometimes things are carried out differently by the will of God.

The thing that pains me the most is that, when I spoke to him the night before he passed, that was the man I always wished I knew.

I still thank God for Joseph, every day, because he chose me as his son and saved me from being raised by the system. It completely crushed me to lose Joseph, but it also helped me to find my own calling.

With each day that goes by, I pray that he is proud of me and I believe that he is. I understand that, sometimes the world puts a lot on our shoulders, and sometimes we feel that we cannot bear it.

I only wish that I could go back and help you to not give up, so long ago. From all of the great stories I've heard, you were one heck of a man.

Another thing that pains me is that it took so many years for you and me to make a great moment, that would only last a few hours, but it was a time I will never forget.

After you passed it took me five long years of grieving to let go.

I have a great love for you Joseph, and I hope you know that you helped me to keep moving forward towards my dreams.

I send prayers up to heaven asking for your thoughts. I always hoped that I would make you proud of me and you gave me the closure I needed on the day you passed on. Your wonderful parting words to me were "I'm so proud of you. I love you my baby boy…… baby boy!"

I hope you hold my hand as I walk my path. Let me just say, Joseph Munafo, you will always be a great man no matter what, and trust me, we all have our flaws, my father.

You became an idol to me and I've heard so many great stories that let me know you were a rock star!

A few years after my mom and Joseph severed their relationship, she began a new life with my current step dad, Jimmy.

He ended up raising me, being a great role model and a wonderful example of a real dad.

Growing up, I had pretty much all the toys a kid could possibly want, so I definitely had an active imagination.

I remember, around the age of five, I used to love sitting in front of the television with a spoon and singing along with my favorite shows like Sesame Street, and He-Man.

My parents would let me sit there and sing all day if I wanted to. In my opinion it's very important to allow children to express their unique creativity, that's how they find their path to happiness in life.

Sitting there with that spoon all day may have been a sign for my future, because today I run a wonderful business that revolves around the best food made for a spoon - and that, of course, is ice cream.

My humble beginnings definitely helped to mold me into the man I am today.

I don't want to be too nostalgic, but sometimes, in order to truly find yourself, you have to get back to the basics, or should I say the beginnings, whether they are sweet and fruitful or traumatizing and not quite understandable.

DOMINIC MUNAFO

My mom, my wife and Jimmy on my mom's 60th birthday

Sometime between the age of three and five, I had an unfortunate accident happen to me. I fell down a few steps, landing on an old oil can, which actually went through the skin of my hand, luckily, not all the way through to the other side.

The oil caused an infection and the doctors were considering amputating my hand if the infection had spread. I had to get stitched up, but my mom said that I fought those doctors with the strength of six humans.

I remain scarred to this day, but it reminds me of Jesus every time I look at it.

Life may not always be a bed of roses, but I've learned that, if you consider the true lessons of your past, you will learn to appreciate it.

That is very true of my understanding about being adopted. It was made clear to me from the beginning that I was adopted, but I have to admit it was a rollercoaster of emotions. I went from feeling happy to sad and back again.

I started bottling up my emotions within. I felt like I had been given up on even before I had a chance. I started to feel that I wasn't good enough and that it was my fault.

My family got me through that, and, over time, I came to see that it wasn't so – but still, sometimes the feelings were there.

I just wanted to take a moment to give you a glimpse into my family and past because even though we sometimes try so hard to forget the past it is still a part of us.

Remember, without our past we would not be who we are today! Don't run from your past, embrace it. We all live to learn and learn to live.

Let me say this, to anyone contemplating Adoption or Foster care, I implore you to do it. There are too many children in the world being raised by the system instead of a loving family.

Our strongest power is love and just by sharing yours with a child in need can change their direction in life.

CHAPTER TWO – GROWING UP

When I was a kid, my uncle Charlie used to watch baseball on television just about every day. I eventually took notice and began to watch, and love, the American pastime just as much as uncle Charlie did.

His favorite team was the Baltimore Orioles and he would sometimes take me to see them play live at Oriole Park at Camden Yards.

Once we were at a game and the 'Iron man' himself, Cal Ripken Jr. hit a ball right down my way. I tried to catch it but the ball tipped off my glove, went two aisles past me and a little girl picked it up. Even though I didn't get to claim the ball for my own, I was still glad to see the look on that little girl's face when she got it.

I realized then that other people's happiness is just as important as my own.

I eventually loved the game so much that I started playing for a small local team, known as North Point Village.

I absolutely loved playing on that team. I played with them for two years and we won a championship as well. Baseball for me became an escape from reality.

All I had to do was get out there, hit the ball and all my troubles seem to disappear.

On top of that, at night I used to put myself to sleep by visualizing that I was playing for the Baltimore Orioles in the World Series.

It would always be game seven, bases loaded, bottom of the ninth, and I'm up to bat.

Of course I score a home run to finish it off and bring the entire team to victory.

I have always loved baseball and, even though I didn't become a famous major league player, the game itself has become a big part of my life, metaphorically speaking.

ADOPTION SAVED MY LIFE

There are a lot of things that are true in baseball, that are true in life – here are some of the ones that I live by:-

- **You have to take each base one at a time before you score.**

- **I always try to hit a homerun with everything I do.**

- **Every "no" is like a strike; just because I got one it doesn't mean the game is over.**

- **Sometimes even a foul ball for me can be a blessing for someone else.**

THE MAGIC OF SURVIVAL

One day that I'll never forget was when I was around thirteen years old. I was on my way, walking down to the baseball field, with my glove and baseball in hand, and I was ready to play.

I happened to look across the street and saw that my cousins Angela and Amanda were selling Girl Scout cookies door to door.

The door that they happened to be knocking on was the home of my soccer coach, Mr. Scott. I wanted to warn them that he wasn't home, so I yelled out, but they couldn't hear me.

So I ran across the street, without thinking and, before I knew it, out of nowhere, I was hit by an oncoming car.

My head smashed into the windshield, I was thrown into the air, and I landed halfway under another car, about 50 feet away. I was hit so hard that it literally knocked me out of my shoes and I still have the dents, in the back of my head, to prove it.

They had to have me airlifted, by helicopter, to the shock trauma center.

I ended up with a few cracked ribs, dents in my head, and a black eye, but I miraculously walked out of that hospital the very next day. Thank God

Another hard lesson that I faced was also at around the age of 13, when I fell victim to alcohol poisoning. At this time I was staying with my aunt Mary and her husband Nelson. One day, while I was hanging with a friend, his mom gave us some alcohol and, in my ignorance, I guzzled it down with some Kool-Aid.

I ended up passing out on the sidewalk outside, but somehow, I don't know how, as I have no memory of it, I made it back to Aunt Mary's house.

Once I got there, I tried to sober up by taking a shower, but of course that did nothing. My other cousins laughed at me because I was acting so strangely.

I tried to put both legs in one side of my pants and both arms into one side of my shirt and I was squirming on the floor like a fish. Aunt Mary thought I was high on PCP because I was acting so strange.

But uncle Nelson worked it out fast, and called out to Aunt Mary, in his own broken English:-

"Mary, come get this drunk sunama beach"

Once they'd figured out what was going on, they ended up calling an ambulance to take me to the hospital. During the trip I went in to cardiac arrest and the ambulance had to pull over so that they could pump my chest.

After that, once I was home and back to normal, the kid, whose mom gave us the alcohol, used to gather up his friends, to chase me home every day. He did it because he wondered if we were going to call law enforcement on his mom.

I was never afraid of him but, rather, I was afraid of hurting anyone myself. I came to the early realization that violence solves nothing, so I always turned away from it.

My life has been spared so many times, I have to believe that there is a universal plan for me.

If life gives you second and third chances I implore you to make the best of them. I was a little more stubborn so it took a little longer for me to learn my lesson.

Take your mistakes, learn from them and never allow yourself to become a victim. Instead be a victor and lead by example.

That obviously wasn't enough of a warning for me though, because life gave me another one! Let me fast forward to age 18.

At that time I had a Chevy Cavalier Z-24 and I absolutely loved that car.

I felt like a god when I drove down the street.

At that time of my life I also loved partying and drinking.

That was mistake number one.

I went out with one of my cousin's older friends and I thought that he could handle drinking and driving better than I could, since he was older.

That was mistake number two.

He must have been doing about a hundred down the highway, because the car needed gas and we were out of money. (It doesn't make much sense when I say it now – but we thought it made sense at the time...)

That was mistake number three.

As we got closer to his house he decided to floor the gas pedal in order for us to make it through a traffic light.

That was the biggest mistake of them all.

Out of nowhere, a truck came from the side street and smashed right into my side of the car.

The truck hit my car right in the front tire area.

They told me that, if it had been another split second later, I wouldn't be here to tell this story. In other words, logically I should not be here.

I soon realized just how fortunate I was that my life had been spared and I promised myself that I would never go down that path again.

In those moments when we are confronted with, or come close to, a major tragedy, it becomes a moment of decision.

We can either heed the warning or consider ourselves invincible and keep on testing the limits until our luck runs out.

Please learn from my story, that life is precious and should be treated as such.

LIFE LESSONS

Back when I was younger, and my mom and stepdad were working strenuous hours, I would temporarily stay with my aunt Mary, who I became very close with, as well as my other aunt, Janie. I used to call her "nanny", because I couldn't pronounce her name.

Aunt Janie used to give me whatever I wanted and I could get away with anything when it came to her.

While I was with my aunt Janie I started hanging out with the wrong crowd, then began to act out and cut school. Janie worked third shift overnight, so sometimes, while she slept during the day, I would sneak out of the house, just so I could come walking into the house after she woke up, to make it look like I had been at school.

I got away with it for a while, but little did I know that I would pay for it later. You can't graduate if you're never in school.

In my school years, especially high school, I excelled in certain subjects but in others not so much.

This was not due to a lack of learning capacity - in fact, I have always been very smart. I had the best results with the teachers who were more engaging with their students, because they kept me interested.

My best grades in high school were in science and math. My math teacher, Mr. Moxley, would always teach his kids with laughter and I loved that about him. Laughter is the cure to negative thinking. If you can make someone laugh, you can change the direction of their day.

My science teacher, Mr. Elmer Cook, would always find a way to reward each kid's good work and help them move to the head of the class.

I believe that rewarding should be a part of everyday life. Parents should reward their children for hard work and every good business should reward their employees for their hard work.

During my high school years, I met one of the most challenging moments of my life. I made it all the way to my senior year in 1997, but there were still two classes that I hadn't even completed from 9th, 10th, and 11th grade - Social Studies and English.

The reason for that was not lack of understanding, but lack of application. If you do not apply yourself, your results will reflect that.

The principal called my mom and told her that they did not foresee me completing those by the end of the school year. In that moment of declaration something triggered within me.

I deeply disliked being told that I couldn't, or wouldn't, do something, so it sparked a determination in me to prove them wrong. I took extra night classes, and Saturday classes, to try to improve my situation, all while I was working a day job at Wendy's.

In other words, I finally started applying myself. The next thing I knew the principal was calling my mom again and of course mom was thinking 'Oh no, not again.'

The principal then proceeded to tell her that, not only had I pulled it off and would indeed be graduating, but that I had made the honor roll as well.

Trust me, hard work will always pay off, especially when you are determined. You can do anything that you're determined to do.

You can do anything that you're committed to - you don't even have to wait for a challenge to motivate you.

Prove to yourself that you are capable of great things.

One of my biggest inspirations in life came from a man I've never even met, a man who passed away many years ago, and a man whose legacy still lives on today. This man that inspired me so much was Dave Thomas, the founder of Wendy's restaurants.

I worked there for a year or so. I started in an entry level position, then moved to shift leader, then up to crew chief. I've always been a people person and it has helped me to move up the ladder at pretty much every job I've had.

While at Wendy's, I learned some of the best of entrepreneurship as well.

The business practices, which Mr. Thomas had set in place, taught me the foundation of running a successful business.

They taught me how to give back to the customer, and how to live by inspiring others.

Mr. Thomas was adopted, just like I was, so that gave me another way to relate to him, because he also dedicated his life to bringing something special to the world and he never let anything stop him.

Ultimately, he started an organization called the Dave Thomas foundation, in 1992.

This non-profit organization is dedicated to finding adoptive homes for children waiting in North America's overcrowded foster care system.

Adoption has always been a passion of mine, obviously, because I was adopted and I can relate to the plight of children all over the world, who need loving families and need support.

My wife, Doris, and I hope to adopt a child of our own someday.

Sometimes adopted kids have a bad perception of their situation.

They often feel bad about their birth parents giving them up, but I learned something from Les Brown about seeing that differently.

He said that, at one time he was going on radio shows and other interviews, and speaking negatively about his birth parents for giving him away.

He said that a good friend told him, "You weren't given away; you were simply born into the heart of your adoptive mother."

Adoption doesn't have to be a crutch to support your reason for failure. Let it be the basis for pursuing more.

In 1999 we all moved from Maryland to South Carolina, in search of a new beginning. My stepdad, Jimmy, wanted to start a new business as well.

A friend took him to an ice cream shop, known as Original Painters and, seeing just how busy it was, he put a proposal to the owner, to buy the company.

He got the agreement and purchased the company. Jimmy did the manpower of the business and I took over the company, because of my people skills and experience in business. Jimmy has been an awesome example of following your dreams.

He came to this country from Greece, with only fifty dollars and a dream. He eventually started his own painting business, with two close friends and was very successful with it. Moving from the painting business to Original Painters just seemed to make sense.

I became the face of Original Painters and the company has been a huge blessing to me, not because of money, but because I have made many lasting friendships over the years.

In the movie Forrest Gump, he had a famous line where he said *"life is like a box of chocolates…"*

I say life is like an assortment of roses, you never know each day what color you're going to get.

So many things have happened, since we bought that business. That ice cream shop has been the place where things in my life have changed, and changed again.

One of the most challenging moments came early in us having the shop.

I was 21 when I found my birth mother. We had been in contact with each other, and she had expressed an interest in stopping by my shop, because she was in the area.

The first time I saw her it buckled me. As I looked out of my ice cream parlor, I saw a short lady standing before me.

She had a small child with her, that she seemed to be so protective of, who was apparently her son.

Granted, I have an awesome loving mother of my own and I wouldn't trade her for the world!! But in a weird way, it hurt so much to see this lady standing before me, that had given up on me from day one, yet stood before me with another child who obviously thought she was the mother of the year (and for him, I hope she was).

My emotions were running pretty high that day, but I'm still grateful for meeting her. I've never held any grudges against her and, trust me, all is forgiven.

Think of the world like this:

"You are an artist and you can paint the world any way you see fit"

CHAPTER THREE - THE ICE CREAM KING

People ask me all the time, why my business is so busy?

Why do the people line up each and every day just to have some ice cream?

What is it that makes your product so special?

Sometimes I find myself at a loss for words, but let me try to explain it anyway.

I believe that there are multiple reasons for this; first, I approach my business just like my life, my philosophy is that, if I would not eat it, I will not serve it.

I'm dedicated to providing a great product!

Also every single person that comes to see me knows that they're going to get service with a smile, and I'm going to leave them with a piece of my heart before they go!

When people ask me for advice, the number one thing that I say is that you have to "release yourself" and not worry about how someone else will perceive you.

How you perceive you is most important. If you come from your heart, you can, and will, move mountains.

Also remember that you never know who stands before you, so the average Joe or Jane should be treated the same as your favorite celebrity.

What I mean by this is that people are just that, people!

I used to get star struck when meeting famous people, but I realized that, at the end of the day, they are just people, like you and I.

They deserve the same treatment you would give to the everyday individual!

When it came to seeking customers, any door that I entered, I never went in with the purpose of making them a fan!

I went in strictly with the love I have in my soul for giving them a quality product that speaks for itself.

Darius Rucker from Hootie and the Blowfish with 'The Ice Cream King'

I was definitely born with the gift of the gab, and I always leave the customer with a product, and a business card, with links to social media and how to connect with me.

You can see from that picture just how busy the shop gets – how many customers come, and come back, because not only do I give them a great product, but a great service experience.

I was always told that there was no way I could get my ice cream to the people that I dreamed of and hearing that just pushed me to work harder. And working harder got results.

I have served ice cream to many famous people, including B.B. King, who actually gave me the title "Ice Cream King."

But this is not something that will make you successful overnight! It takes commitment and determination!

#NowThatsTheScoop

I've been blessed to be able to knock down barriers and open doors – doors that I was told were never going to open for me, yet I kept knocking!

I knew that, if my intentions were pure, the world would listen.

Don't get me wrong, I've made some enemies along the way, but my friendships outweigh that at least a thousand to one.

What I mean is that not everybody is going to believe in you, or be a fan, so to speak.

Sometimes people may see you, but still not realize that there are some pretty good people in this world and that you're one of them!

So I'm letting you know that, if you can't handle rejection, maybe you should have someone else handle your business dealings, because rejection is part of the process.

I'm not a person that accepts "no" for an answer and I won't let it get in my way! So if you want the answers I will give you my personal answer; I walk with the man upstairs!

I would never push my beliefs on any man or woman and I also choose not to treat anyone differently, based upon their beliefs.

No matter what our different beliefs are, we all have one thing in common and that is the desire for success in life. Success comes in any language and any culture. If you are willing to work hard, commit, stay focused, and believe in yourself, then success is imminent.

We all walk with our beliefs, and I show love to every single person in this world that blesses me, and my business, with the honor of serving them! I will wash any man or woman's feet that grace my path! Speaking metaphorically of course!

There's only one true answer that I have for you and that is "God Did It." I believe that He will open up doors that you thought couldn't be opened. He can take you from ordinary to extraordinary.

OVERCOME YOUR FEARS

Another close encounter that I had was in 2006, when I crossed the path of a young bull in Cancun, Mexico and we went face to face, toe to toe. My wife and I were at a bull fight arena and they were looking for volunteers to try something crazy.

The next thing I knew my wife was yelling out *"Pick him, pick him."*

I guess my wife thought it was funny to volunteer me to take on a blood thirsty animal.

Thinking back now, she did try to sign me up for life insurance around that same time.

I'm joking of course, but I had the time of my life in that arena. Initially I thought it was a joke and maybe someone would come out in a bull costume.

You can imagine how I almost ruined a pair of pants when I saw the real deal come out of that gate.

It was a terrifying moment, but also a moment I don't regret at all.

It takes guts, and tremendous heart, to take on a fear like that. I was initially scared but I stepped over the threshold of fear and I stood tall.

Every fear faced and released is another step towards success.

And every fear faced makes it easier to face the next one.

ADOPTION SAVED MY LIFE

THIS IS YOUR LIFE CHANGE

One day I found out about a TV show contest, called "This is Your Life Change" that was helping people to pursue their dreams.

They were offering a life changing trip to Fiji for the winners and I wanted in. Thousands of people entered the contest including myself. I made it all the way to the top 50.

Former Dundalk resident looks for help from his home town

Munafo a finalist for "This is Your Life Change" show

By BILL GATES
bgates@chespub.com

Dominic Munafo has the opportunity to change his life. But he needs your help.

"You," in this case, being the residents of his Dundalk home town.

Munafo, a 1997 graduate of Sparrows Point High, has been named one of 50 semifinalists for a reality show called "This is Your Life Change."

Six of those 50 people from across the world will be chosen for a "two-week life-changing trip to Fiji."

Who helps selects the fortunate six? People casting votes at the web site thisisyourlifechange.com (the voting ends on May 30.)

from 60 countries before the field was narrowed to 50 semifinalists.

The 50 semifinalists were chosen based on application videos in which they described their "secret dreams" and explained why they deserved to be selected.

"It's a combination TV show/social experiment," Munafo said. "On Fiji, we'll work with life, business and fitness coaches."

The event is being described as a "lifestyle boot camp" by its creator, Mark Bowness. The six finalists will receive help in launching their business, product or charity, as well as support for a year after the end of the two weeks in Fiji.

Specifically, the camp will be held on the island of Vorovoro, a 200-acre volcanic island that is part of the Fiji chain. For those two weeks, the six

that are waiting for someone to call mommy and daddy."

Munafo also wants to be able to provide counseling for adopted children.

"If you believe in me, please vote," Munafo said. "I'm setting out to change the world, but no one can change the world without help from others.

"I've always had love for my home town. Now I'm asking for the help of my home town."

Online voting will be accepted through May 30. Three finalists will be chosen by the voting; the other three will be chosen by Bowness and and his This is Your Life Change team.

Another of his goals is to help his parents.

"I want to be able to set my parents up financially to where they can comfortably

41

After I entered the contest, my hometown newspaper back in Maryland, The Dundalk Eagle, did a story about me being in the top 50 contestants, in order to rally support for me. On the previous page you can see a clip from their article.

I was so humbled by their reaction, because that was the very place where I had learned to be the man that I am today. I also made many lasting friendships there.

Although I didn't win the contest, it was still amazing knowing that I was pursuing my dreams and I never stopped. Anytime there's an opportunity to pursue your dreams, take it. Anytime there's an opportunity to speak your voice, then do it loud and proud.

The road is never easy but the rewards are indescribable.

CHAPTER FOUR – DOMINIC'S NOTEBOOK

"The day has arrived; a moment that I will be most proud of in my life is upon us. Dominic's Notebook is hereby official as a non-profit organization, a 501 (c) (3). It is so amazing to turn a childhood dream of mine into a reality, and the greatest gift of it all is to be able to make a difference in countless lives hopefully all over the world!"

January 28th 2016 (Facebook post)

For a long time I prayed, contemplated, and debated within myself on how I could help make a difference in the world. I wondered what I could do, to contribute to something worthwhile. Dominic's Notebook© was the answer to my prayers.

Have you ever found yourself so afraid of the unknown, not because you won't succeed, but because, without others, your dreams are merely just that, a dream?

I've found something in life that honestly outweighs me. This is a moment in time that is so important, that I feel the hardest pressure on me, but in a good way.

I know deep down at this moment, that I cannot, and will not, fail, simply because this moment was delivered to me by God and I believe that I am working one of his gifts!

As you know, not all children get the opportunity to be adopted. I thought to myself that there's no way I can get every child in this world adopted so, how can I give back? How can I make a difference for these great children?

The answer came to me in the form of Dominic's Notebook.

Dominic's Notebook is an official non-profit organization that supports kids and young adults, with school supplies and other every day needs.

This organization is now in its infancy but our aim is to maximize its capacity for outreach support to kids all over the country, and eventually the world.

Dominic's Notebook collects and donates essential school supplies to the people and places where they are needed most.

The goal of this organization is to provide help to kids in general, and, in particular, to young adults who get emancipated from foster care system, but lack the everyday guidance and resources available to the rest of us.

Oftentimes these kids are sent out into the world without any sort of plan of action and we, as an organization, want to help them, by developing an adult life plan that guides and supports them.

Our intent is to design a program, with specific guidelines and rules, in order to provide resources such as counseling, help with job placement, housing, and even access to further education.

Dominic's Notebook means more to me than anything I've ever done! It's that moment in life where you feel tears of joy, tears of success! It's the moment I've spent my entire life searching for.

We all have our destinies, and it's amazing, yet scary to know that I can't sink with this one, I have to succeed!

So many lives depend on this very moment, so many children need this great gift.

I started Dominic's Notebook to turn a dream into a reality and I also started it for the sake of my mother, Cheryl Munafo.

In all honesty, one of the main reasons Dominic's Notebook was created was to show my mother just how much she impacted my life. I wanted to show her that it takes a real woman to raise a child and not just to make one.

One of the things my mother always told me was the importance of an education, and how I needed college in order to succeed - to some degree she is correct.

However there are a small percentage of people that still achieve high success with maximized effort, regardless of not having that college education and, thanks to my stepfather Jimmy, the only real man I ever knew as a dad, I'm part of that small percentage.

But think about the children who slip through the cracks, who never have a chance to call someone mom and dad - the best chance that they have to succeed is an education, and that's why Dominic's Notebook© was created.

I want to give the children of tomorrow that chance at a life they deserve. Know that, when you donate to our organization, every cent given goes towards making that happen.

CNN reported in 2014 that, each year, over 23,000 kids are "emancipated" or "aged out" of the foster care system at age 18. In other words, they are released into the world because the state (by law) can no longer house them. These kids are usually sent out with no housing and no emotional or financial support.

You can find the report here:-

http://www.cnn.com/2014/04/16/opinion/soronen-foster-children/index.html

These statistics are the main reason why the world can benefit from Dominic's Notebook©.

You may think to yourself; how is a pencil or a piece of paper going to make a difference? How can this foundation make any sort of impact?

Fostering Success in Education:
National Factsheet on the Educational Outcomes of Children in Foster Care

January 2014

Why Education Matters to Children in Foster Care

When supported by strong practices and policies, positive school experiences can counteract the negative effects of abuse, neglect, separation, and lack of permanency experienced by the nearly 400,000 U.S. children and youth in foster care. Education not only supports economic success in adult life, it also provides opportunities for improved well-being in physical, intellectual, and social domains during critical developmental periods. A concerted effort by child welfare agencies, education agencies, and the courts could lead to significant progress in changing the consistent and disheartening picture the research portrays. The promising programs and interventions highlighted below represent innovative efforts to address a wide range of factors influencing the disparities in education outcomes. With cross-system collaboration, we are positioned to build on what is being learned, bring about change, and promote success for all children and youth in foster care.

Fast facts from national and multi-state studies*

Number of children and youth in foster care on September 30, 2012	399,546
Average number of living arrangements during first foster care stay	2.8
Number of foster children of school age	249,107
Likelihood of being absent from school	2x that of other students
Percent of foster youth who change schools when first entering care	56%-75%
Percent of 17-18 year olds in care who have experienced 5+ school changes	34%
Likelihood of 17-18 year old foster youth having an out-of-school suspension	2x that of other students
Likelihood of 17-18 year old foster youth being expelled	3x that of other students
Average reading level of 17-18 year olds in foster care	7th grade
Likelihood of foster youth receiving special education	2.5 - 3.5x that of others
Percent of foster youth who complete high school by 18	50%
Percent of 17-18 year old foster youth who want to go to college	84%
Percent of foster youth who graduated from high school who attend college	20%
Percent of former foster youth who attain a bachelor's degree	2 - 9%

*All fast facts are referenced elsewhere in this document. These facts were compiled based on findings from multiple studies where a consistent picture is emerging that points to widespread deficits on a number of markers of educational progress or success. Data points represented here are either from national studies or multiple studies conducted in different states (in which case a range is provided for the data point).

The way we will do that is by bringing awareness to these subpar statistics. We will also do that by being a helping hand with every day resources.

Government funding for education is extremely below where it needs to be, so I encourage you all to support organizations like Dominic's Notebook© to help make a difference.

On average there are over 400,000 children in foster care in the United States every year! Of the 400,000 a little more than half may return to their home environment, over 184,000 remain in the system each year and 10% on average stay in foster care until the age of 18.

Of that 10% the majority of these children drop out of school, end up pregnant, or into drugs etc.

Dominic's Notebook hopes to help change these statistics by not only supplying school supplies, but by being vocal throughout the world, sharing these staggering statistics.

So can we make a difference? I say yes we can and, over time, we will.

I was fortunate enough to leave foster care as early as 14 months old, but many children are not as fortunate. Now I want to pay forward the same type of love I was given. As for my mom, Cheryl Munafo, thank you for inspiring me to want to give a piece of that love, which you gave me, to someone else.

You're my idol! Love you Mom!

To anyone reading this, know that your greatest gift is not for you. It has been given to you in order for you to give it to others. In life I have found that your talents will make you money, but your gifts will make you happy.

Don't allow yourself to question it, just know that you must pay it forward for the greater good. When you seek to do good, then goodness will seek you as well.

Many years ago, a man I knew taught me a saying that goes *"One hand washes the other, two wash the face"* and it basically means, I help you, you help me.

To me it also means one hand belongs to us and the other belongs to our peers. When you contribute to others, think of it as adding muscle to them.

You're not just supporting them, you're strengthening them. What you contribute to them will also inspire them.

Allow yourself to be inspired by others so that you may one day pay that same energy forward and be inspirational to someone else.

Here's a donation given to Dominic's Notebook by my good friend Mark Penn.

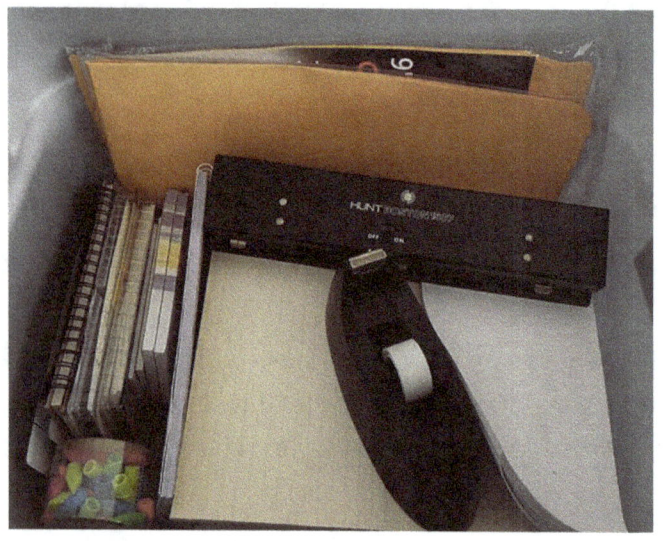

I celebrate people like Mark because they have, voluntarily, taken from their own just to help someone else in need.

Your greatest gift will always contribute to someone in some way. I cannot even begin to stress to you how important it is to find your gift in this world.

If you're saying to yourself that you don't have a gift, well you're wrong.

You just haven't found it yet. Keep searching, keep knocking, keep asking and your gift will soon be revealed to you.

Future dreams become present facts.

To those with a dream, I implore you not to give up on it.

No matter how long it takes, know that <u>it is possible</u> and that <u>it is possible for you</u>.

Some people sit around waiting for things to happen and some people stand up and make them happen.

Today I stand proud as all of my dreams are becoming a reality, let this show you that all your dreams are held in your palms, all you have to do is make them happen!

Stand up and make yourself accountable for your own actions.

You control the message you wish to deliver. Grasp your opportunities and make them prosper.

We can all sit around and talk about "what if" and "what could have been," but today can be the day we all make it happen!

At the same time this book is being written, we are in the process of hosting a celebrity golf tournament and celebrity wrestling event, called "Ice Cream Mania", for the fall of 2016.

All the proceeds will be donated directly to Dominic's Notebook in order to help kids in need. I hope that, by the time you read this book, we have scored a hole in one with support for this event.

"Our rewards in life will always be in exact proportion to our contribution, our service"

- Earl Nightingale

SUPPORT FOR DOMINIC'S NOTEBOOK

From the start, the Dominic's Notebook project has had some incredible support, from some amazing people – here's just a few examples.

A visit from my good friend Vanna White in support of Dominic's Notebook!

#NowThatsTheScoop

One of my friends, James Michael Sheppard, gave his own personal, heartfelt video testimony about my work with Dominic's Notebook - here's what he had to say.

https://www.facebook.com/James.Michael.Sheppard/videos/453923438149909/

> "This is James and I'm bringing you this video because I was really touched this morning. Dominic Munafo put out a video this morning….he's doing everything he can to try and make a better world for these foster kids. I'm asking that you guys go to his page and share his stuff, because that's all it takes is one person to share the right video and it can set brand new dreams for these kids and make them more successful than anything we've ever dreamed of being, simply by having the essential necessities for when they walk out of their house…. that they feel successful in who they are.

Whether it be their clothes, car or where they stay. These kids have to have some kind of backing and confidence in who they are so they can be successful, and that's exactly what Dominic Munafo is trying to do…..and it doesn't take much. It takes a little share of a video or a little kind heart."

- James M. Sheppard

I want to thank James, and anyone else, who supports my mission to help and raise awareness for children in need.

We can't save the entire world by ourselves, but we can do our part.

CHAPTER FIVE – LIVE YOUR DREAMS

Someone in the world needs to hear your story.

Remember, every one of you possess the capability of greatness! It's all up to you to go after what you want out of life! Nothing is given to us without earning it, and earning it never comes easy!

Sometimes it feels as if no one is listening and no one is watching, but don't worry, just keep going forward with strict persistence. It takes blood, sweat, and tears to get to what you want! Whatever you seek in this world is achievable, if you are willing to fight for it and never give up. I once heard Tyler Perry say that "sometimes you're meant to be hidden".

He explained that sometimes God will keep you hidden below the radar, in order for you to have an even greater impact on the world.

He said that, in the beginning no one would pay attention to his work and because of that, his competition underestimated him. I love it when people underestimate me, because it gives me more fuel to get fired up.

When the time is right, God will unleash your presence on the world. Keep asking, keep knocking, keep believing, and keep your patience.

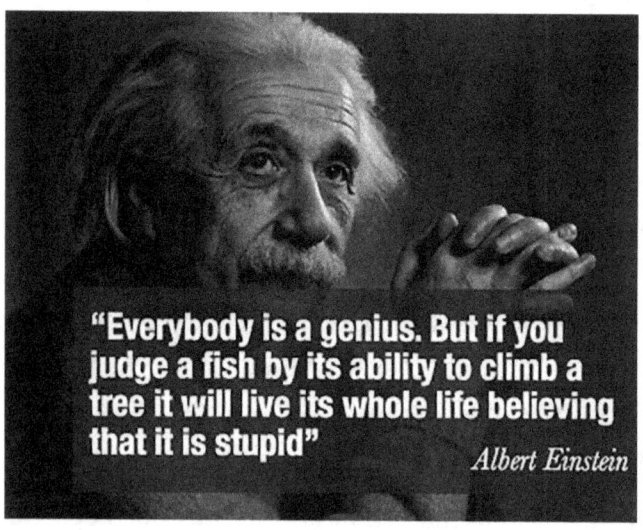

Remember, in life praise is not always going to come, but know in your heart that what you're doing truly makes a difference, sometimes we have to hit multiple home runs before our peers take notice.

Walk the earth like an individual with a strong message to deliver and give the world a reason to appreciate you.

We walk among millions, but remember, we each possess a unique gift that no one else has; the key is learning how to tap into that gift and never letting anything or anyone get in the way!

Find your gifts, deliver them to the world and let nothing stop you. Hard work and determination will always prosper, trust me I see improvement in myself every day, and in those around me.

Failure is nothing more than a side effect of laziness, when your efforts are low, but success shall always come to any person that fights for it.

Many of us sit around and bicker about the choices that we have to make each day, and the work that sits before us. What if you had to say goodbye today?

Would you be proud of the life you've lived?

"Your gifts are as unique as your fingerprints"

– Curtis Florence

It's never too late to realize that we all have blessings and gifts. We are supposed to leave an impact on this world, far beyond our time!!

What's your message, what do you want to leave to tomorrow when tomorrow has passed us by?

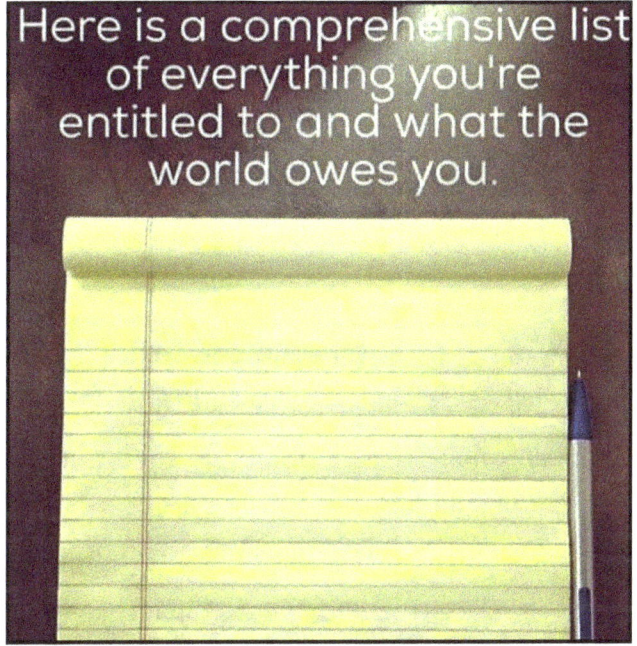

Because of my desire to follow my dreams and make a difference I never gave up on it.

I knew that it would take some time, but I made a decision that I would bring it to reality, no matter how long it took.

My dream was to bring a nonprofit organization to the world that would help kids, and I have now achieved that. Reach down deep within yourself and pull out your secret dream.

Trust me it's there, you just have to unleash it. In the beginning tell no one, while you work on it, so that no one will attempt to talk you out of it. When the time is right unleash your dream on the world. Work day and night on it, and dream day and night about it.

Because of my hard work and persistence I've had the privilege of serving many celebrities at my shop.

The main thing I have found is that they are everyday people just like you and I but it has still been a great experience doing it.

I have served ice cream to famous rappers like Waka Flocka, Mac Miller, and other musicians like Darius Rucker, B.B. King, Mike Love from the Beach Boys and Puddle of Mudd. Famous comedians like Dave Chappelle and Carlos Mencia.

TV personalities like Vanna White, Willie from Duck Dynasty, and Meteorologist Jim Cantore.

"Dream lofty dreams and as you dream so shall you become. Your vision is the promise of what you shall one day be; your ideal is the prophecy of what you shall at last unveil"

– James Allen

I've served sports personalities like Ron Devine and Ric Flair just to name a few.

Meeting celebrities is always amazing, and I've got so many great memories (and the pictures to go with them!). Here is the Nature boy, Ric Flair and I after he almost beat me up twice. LOL

The first time he got mad because I asked if Hulk Hogan was the actual owner of TNA Wrestling. The second time was when I asked a lady to take a picture of him and me only to find out that she was his wife and he almost gave me a Flair Chop.

I always enjoy myself and I've had some amazing opportunities! (this shot was taken when I appeared on TV)

THANK YOU

I would like to extend my deepest and most sincere gratitude to the many people who have helped make me who I am today.

I could not have delivered this message without your personal touch on my life.

First and foremost, I thank God for giving me life. I thank my birth parents for being the vessels for my entrance into this world.

I owe a debt of gratitude to my adoptive parents, Joseph and Cheryl Munafo, for choosing me and giving me a wonderful start.

To my mom Cheryl, I will say this again; you are truly amazing and it takes a real woman to raise a child, not just to have one.

To Joseph, I thank you every day for choosing me as your own son and starting me on the path to greatness.

To the only man that I say I love more than a father, my stepdad Jimmy, you will always be my Dad and you will always be a man I pray to be like.

I know that I've hurt you at times, but I love you more than anything. You are a huge inspiration to me and I hope that I have made you proud. You are one of my best friends.

To my wife, Doris Munafo, you give me the inspiration to keep moving forward even when people try to knock me down. Thank you for all of your love and thanks for letting me know that I can do anything I set out to do. You are my rock and my heart place. You complete me and you are my true best friend.

You put up with all of my "stuff" and I can share anything with you without worrying about judgement. You inspire me, because I learn just how great you are every day.

I admire you and I have the utmost respect for you. The happiest day for me was when you became Mrs. Dominic Munafo.

I'm the luckiest man on the planet thanks to you.

I love you Doris Munafo.

TO MY WIFE

We have been through so many ups and downs

So much love and so many frowns

You've stuck with me when no one else would

I've tried to give you all of the love I could

You're an inspiration because you make me feel that way

I thank God for you each and every day

You lifted me up when I felt incomplete

You guide me like your controlling my feet

You're one of the greatest, a true inspiration

Doris Herring became Doris Munafo for a reason.

Fourteen years and I still love you like day one

Even when it's raining you provide me with the sun

You rock my world with your smile and grace

I don't think I've ever seen a more beautiful face

You turn my world upside down

Each day I walk with you, trust me, I can't frown

You're one of the most beautiful, sincere, and great

I've loved you ever since we had our first date

A special thank you goes to my cousin Chuck Freburger for supporting and loving me like your own brother. I'm so honored that you would take time out of your life to help support Dominic's Notebook which is something that means more to me than anything I've ever accomplished. I admire all of your hard work and I love you my brother!

Thank you to all of my grandparents for everything you did for the family.

To Mr. Ron Devine and BK Racing, I have been blessed to see your family grow over the years and to have you all as part of my extended family. I'm not sure what you saw in me but I thank you from the bottom of my heart for everything you helped me to accomplish. You are a true role model and a great individual that I am proud to say is my friend. The one moment I remember the most was when I first met you at my ice cream shop and I jokingly said *"Hi, welcome to Burger King!"*

From that day on we made quite the friendship. It was such an ironic moment when I found out that you actually were a Burger King Franchise owner. It has been a true blessing to have you as a friend and to see your family grow. You do great things for this world and I am extremely proud of you.

Thanks to Mr. Ron Devine and BK racing, my company logo can be seen on a NASCAR vehicle. Never could I have imagined that, one day, I would even be in the company of someone like J.J. Yeley, not to mention seeing my logo on a car that he's been in.   **#DreamsComeTrue**

Thank you to my Aunt Mary, tricky Nicky loves you forever. I know I put you through hell, but I thank you for not giving up on me. You were like a second mother to me and I'll never forget everything you did for me.

Thank you my late Aunts Charity, Jean, and Janie. You all have made a special impact on my life, more than anyone will ever know.

Thank you to my Uncle Sonny and Aunt Lily.

Thank you to my cousin Mike Caviness. I just want to say keep your head up and keep moving forward. I love you and I'm proud of you.

Thank you to my cousin Carmen and your husband Jerry. Thank you for saving my life on numerous occasions. If it wasn't for the great gifts you gave me, I wouldn't be able to do this.

Thank you to Pam Lund and the Baltimore Ravens. Pam, I want to thank you for your friendship, from the bottom of my heart. It's always great to see your smile when you come to visit. I thank you for all of the gifts that you've given me, throughout my life.

It has been a true blessing to see your family grow up throughout the years. You have a special place in my heart.

To the Baltimore Ravens, thank you for donating to my foundation, and thank you for allowing me on the field as a special guest in 2014, when the Baltimore Ravens played the Carolina Panthers. #GoRavens

Thank you to my good friend Vanna White. Many people know you as a popular television personality, but I know you as a dear friend. You've been a true blessing in my life and I admire the person that you are. What most people don't know about Vanna is that she would give the shirt off of her back to help someone in need. She loves all people and I hope to be like her one day. I also want to thank her brother Chip White. He and I have developed a great bond and friendship.

Thank you to Mr. Jim Cantore - Jim came to my shop and actually scooped ice cream like he was me. I was very touched by what you did. I have a lot of respect for you and I thank you for the service you provide and how you keep us safe.

Thank you to Carl Michael. You are a great magician but I especially thank you for teaching me the magic of life. Also, thank you to another great magician, Bryan Saint. You use magic and comedy to change the world and you definitely changed mine.

Thank you to Aaron Lucas, my videographer. Without you I wouldn't have been able to do my video for "This is your life change".

Thank you to Montell Jordan for allowing me to share my love of ice cream with you. Thank you for becoming a believer and a fan of my product. I am your true friend, because you inspire me with you love for God.

Thank you to my good friend, and Emmy award winner, Justin Wheelon. I'm so proud of you. Your achievements make me strive to be better

Thank you to the star of "Myrtle Manor", Taylor Burt.

Thank you to the winner of Redneck Island, Jeremy Morris.

Thank you to Keith Mark and Shawn Michaels for inspiring my Mocha Mousse flavor.

Thank you to Sparrows Point High School for the wonderful years. I'm Pointer strong forever. Shout out to the class of 1997.

I want to take a minute to thank all of the board members of Dominic's Notebook©.

These great individuals have blessed me by sitting on the board for Dominic's Notebook© and I couldn't be blessed with a better team.

- Cheryl Munafo this foundation came about thanks to your love and devotion to be the best possible mother and role model a man could ever have and hope for
- my wife Doris Munafo,
- my step dad Jimmy, and
- my cousin Chuck Freburger
- Trina Fields

You are very important people in my life as you help me take on the task of building Dominic's Notebook into an organization that the world will grow to know.

Thank you all for supporting me.

Thank you all for believing in a dream, which was thought of so long ago, a dream that is now reality, thanks to some pretty amazing people!

Thank you to Curtis Florence for believing in me and for taking time to help me with my dream. You are a true inspiration and a great author. I encourage everyone to read Curtis's writings.

Thank you also to Kim Lambert for giving her time and professional expertise, to make this book the best, most polished presentation it could be.

Thanks to the haters. Keep doing what you're doing because it makes me stronger. Keep hating while the rest of the world keeps succeeding.

Last, but not least, thank you to any, and every, one I may have neglected to mention. You all have helped me become the man I am today.

Yours Truly

Dominic Munafo

ADOPTION SAVED MY LIFE

ABOUT THE AUTHOR

Whilst this book is, in essence, all about the author, here is a more compact description!

Dominic Munafo is a loving husband, devoted son, entrepreneur and philanthropist. He owns an extremely successful ice cream business in North Myrtle Beach SC and has founded a nonprofit organization, called Dominic's Notebook, which donates school supplies, and other everyday needs, to kids all over the USA.

Those who know him say he has a heart of gold and only wishes to make a difference in other people's lives.

All profits from this book go to the Dominic's Notebook Foundation.

See the section at the end of the book for how YOU can help!

CONNECT WITH DOMINIC

Twitter	@originalcream26 @DominicsNotebo1
Facebook	https://www.facebook.com/dominic.munafo https://www.facebook.com/Dominics-Notebook-1520873618217868/
Instagram	@originalpainters
Email	dominicsnotebook@outlook.com
Web	find his website at http://dominicsnotebook.org www.theicecreamking.com

HOW YOU CAN HELP DOMINIC'S NOTEBOOK

To anyone reading this book, I ask for your help in my noble cause.

Dominic's Notebook has received so much love and support from the very start, but the number of children in need is growing at rates faster than ever.

I ask you to donate for a child in need to help make a difference.

You may send school supplies, or any everyday items that are in good condition, to 2403 Hilton Dr, North Myrtle Beach, SC 29582 or you can donate monetarily at

https://www.gofundme.com/ehxgeeuk

or through PayPal using email

Dominicsnotebook@outlook.com

If you are from a business that deals in office supplies or similar, we would love to talk to you about how you can become a sponsor – please email us to start the discussion.

DOMINIC MUNAFO

www.ingramcontent.com/pod-product-compliance
Lightning Source LLC
Chambersburg PA
CBHW071010080526
44587CB00015B/2416